Eye-Popping

Popping

OPTICAL

ILLUSIONS

Michael A. DiSpezio

Sterling Publishing Co., Inc.
New York

ACKNOWLEDGMENTS

Once again I have the privilege of being profiled as an author. All books showcase the talent, dedication, and trust of an anonymous army working behind the scenes. My support team begins with Sheila Barry. Her trust in my product proposals gets me into the lineup. Then I'm hooked up with a very special, talented, and dedicated friend, Hazel Chan. Hazel has been my editor on ten Sterling publications. Ten! It's been a treat. In addition to her editing prowess, Hazel facilitates the layout and graphics integration by working with artists Myron Miller and Jeff Ward. Myron's humorous and humanist outlook brings a special comic edge to the book's visuals. Jeff's fine graphics account for much of the magic that pops from these pages. Liz Trovato adds her own imaginative flair in laying out these pages in an attractive and appealing style. And finally, let me not forget the special talent and artistic eye of the book's stereophotographer, Tony DiSpezio. To these masters, I am indebted. Thanks!

Library of Congress Cataloging-in-Publication Data

10 9 8 7 6 5 4 3 2 1

DiSpezio, Michael A.
      Eye-popping optical illusions / Michael A. DiSpezio.
          p. cm.
      Includes index.
      ISBN 0-8069-6641-6
      1. Optical illusions—Juvenile literature. [1. Optical illusions.] I. Title.
QP495 .D573 2000
152.14'8–150>dc21   00-058319

Published by Sterling Publishing Company, Inc.
387 Park Avenue South, New York, N.Y. 10016
©2001 by Michael A. DiSpezio
Distributed in Canada by Sterling Publishing
c/o Canadian Manda Group, One Atlantic Avenue, Suite 105
Toronto, Ontario, Canada M6K 3E7
Distributed in Great Britain and Europe by Chris Lloyd
463 Ashley Road, Parkstone, Poole, Dorset, BH14 0AX, England
Distributed in Australia by Capricorn Link (Australia) Pty Ltd.
P.O. Box 6651, Baulkham Hills, Business Centre, NSW 2153, Australia

Printed in China

Sterling ISBN 0–8069–6641–6

Permissions for Eye-Popping Optical Illusions: Page 40–41, Moon's surface courtesy of NASA; Page 73, all stereophotos courtesy of Tony DiSpezio; Page 74, Golden Gate Bridge anaglyph by Jim Crowell; Page 78, satellite view of Pasadena courtesy of NASA/JPL/Caltech; Page 79, springtail anaglyph: 3-D by David Burder.

CONTENTS

Introduction

Welcome back. This book is the follow-up to OPTICAL ILLUSION MAGIC. If you have the first book, you know what to expect: eye-popping illusions, mind-boggling tricks, bad jokes, and simple explanations of illusion science.

But suppose you don't have the first book? Will you miss out on understanding the science and magic of these optical tricks? No way. Each book is written so that it can "stand alone."

In this book, we will play with your perception, help you make optical illusion devices, and even give you a glimpse of the moon.

Enough words. Let the trickery begin!

THE ADVENTURE CONTINUES

An Overwelming Response

Sights. Sounds. Smells. Your brain is constantly bombarded with all sorts of sensations. The amount of data is overwhelming. In fact, the only way to deal with this continual flood of information is to apply shortcuts. Some of these shortcuts are learned; they come from your everyday experiences. Other shortcuts are "hardwired"; they are part of the brain's natural way of sorting through information.

Most of the time the shortcuts work fine. They filter out "garbage" and allow your brain to spend time on the important things.

Sometimes, however, the shortcuts can lead you astray. They set the scene for "jumping" to wrong comparisons and conclusions. These misguided thoughts form the basis of what we call an optical illusion.

Blasts from the Past

To get you in the mood (and review some of what you already know about optical illusions), let's start off with this quick quiz. Although the concepts may be familiar to those who own OPTICAL ILLUSION MAGIC, the targets are brand new. So take your time and savor these ocular appetizers.

AFTERIMAGE

Make a guess. Before you stare at this afterimage illusion, predict the shape and color of the image that it will create. Once you've made your prediction, stare at the center of the cross for 10 seconds. Then quickly shift your gaze to the center of the blank space at the right. What do you see?

 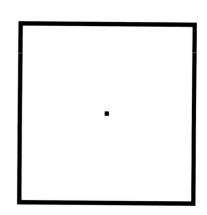

The image that materializes is called an "afterimage." Afterimages result from oversaturating your vision. You can do this by staring at a target for a long time or observing a quick but intense light (as in a camera flash). As your eye recovers from this excess sensation, you'll observe similar shapes, but in complementary colors.

TALL TALE Look at the two red bars below. Sure, one appears longer, but by how much?

a) Same size   b) ▬   c) ▬   d) ▬

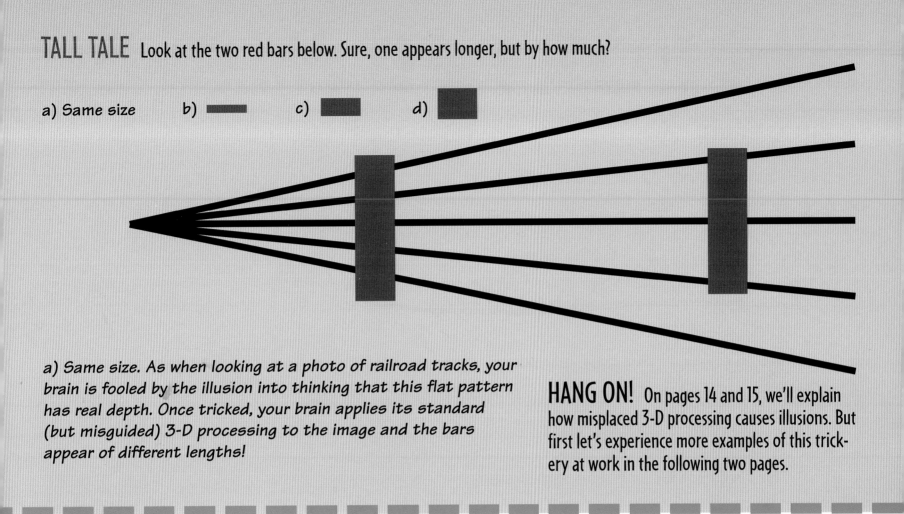

a) Same size. As when looking at a photo of railroad tracks, your brain is fooled by the illusion into thinking that this flat pattern has real depth. Once tricked, your brain applies its standard (but misguided) 3-D processing to the image and the bars appear of different lengths!

HANG ON! On pages 14 and 15, we'll explain how misplaced 3-D processing causes illusions. But first let's experience more examples of this trickery at work in the following two pages.

BAR BRAIN

Compare these two red lines. How much longer is the bottom line than the upper one?

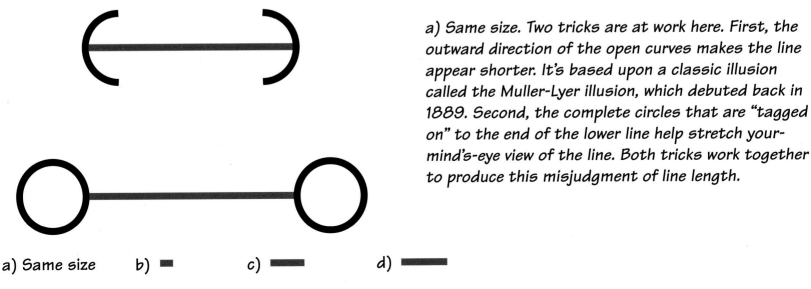

a) Same size. Two tricks are at work here. First, the outward direction of the open curves makes the line appear shorter. It's based upon a classic illusion called the Muller-Lyer illusion, which debuted back in 1889. Second, the complete circles that are "tagged on" to the end of the lower line help stretch your-mind's-eye view of the line. Both tricks work together to produce this misjudgment of line length.

a) Same size   b) ▪   c) ▬   d) ▬

DISTORTED VIEWS

BRAIN DISCLAIMER

Psychologists often don't agree on how an illusion works. In fact, many illusions (even those that have been around for over 100 years) remain somewhat of a mystery. Some scientists believe that an effect is caused by chemical reactions in the eye. Other scientists believe that the same effect is produced by the way nerve messages interfere with each other. Still others believe that faulty shortcuts in thinking may account for the foolery.

On these two pages you'll uncover an assortment of illusions. See if you agree with the explanations behind them. Can you come up with better ones?

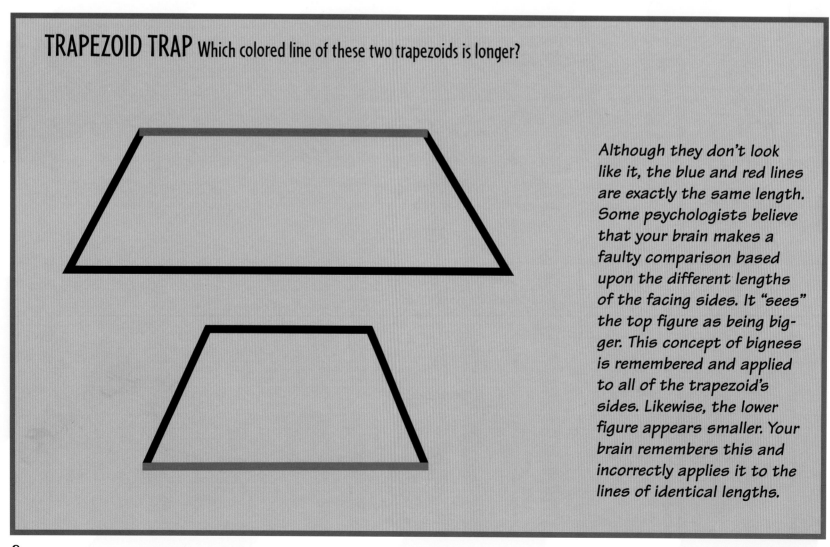

TRAPEZOID TRAP Which colored line of these two trapezoids is longer?

Although they don't look like it, the blue and red lines are exactly the same length. Some psychologists believe that your brain makes a faulty comparison based upon the different lengths of the facing sides. It "sees" the top figure as being bigger. This concept of bigness is remembered and applied to all of the trapezoid's sides. Likewise, the lower figure appears smaller. Your brain remembers this and incorrectly applies it to the lines of identical lengths.

SLANTS ON THE SIDE

Position this illusion so that you aren't looking directly down at it. Just shift the page to the right or left. What appears to happen to the vertical columns when you look at them from an increasing angle?

As you look from the side, the columns appear to spread apart at the top and come together, or converge, at the bottom. The effect is most likely caused by the false sense of 3-D suggested by the slanted lines in the columns. Your brain accepts this trick and wrongly applies 3-D processing.

As your viewing angle increases, the effect intensifies. This may occur from the more convincing "fake-out" created by observing the slanted lines at an angle.

WRECKED RECTANGLE

Is this a perfect red rectangle?

This is a perfectly perfect rectangle. These slanted lines create a disturbing pattern that tricks your brain into applying some unnecessary and image altering 3-D processing. Try moving your viewing angle to either side. How does this affect the strength of the illusion?

SQUARE DEAL?

Can you believe that these two squares are the exact same size?

Only kidding. The square on the right is bigger. We thought we'd include this comparison to keep you guessing on line lengths and shape distortions.

MORE TWISTS

IT'S HIP TO BE SQUARE Now here's another square illusion—or is it? Is the red square a regular square or does it seem to have wider "hips"?

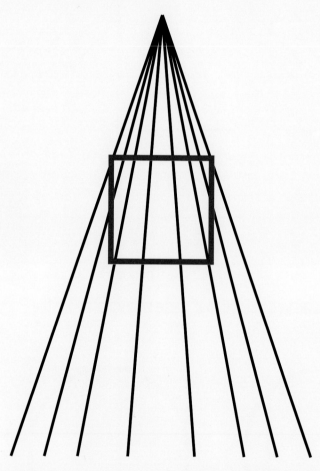

DOTS ON THE SPOT Are the green spots placed in two straight lines or do they jog in and out of the line?

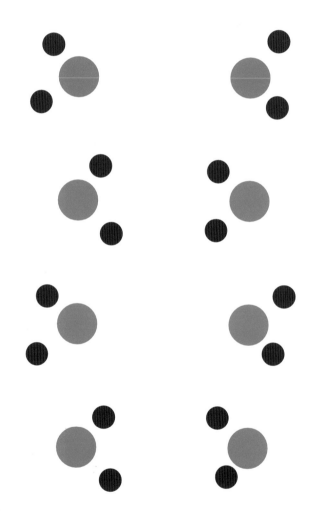

It's a regular square. Just use a straightedge to block off the confounding pattern of lines and you'll discover a shape that has straight sides and right angles. The angled lines strongly suggest a 3-D scene upon which a frame has been placed. Your brain does the rest and "stretches" the upper side.

The green dots are positioned along two parallel lines. There's no jogging here. The illusion is created by the extra spots that appear to stretch and shrink the line segments. Since the alternating segments appear to be different lengths, your brain assumes that the green spots aren't in line.

MAKE A GUESS What color dot is in the middle of the green line?

Would you believe that the red dot is at the midway point? If you must, use a ruler to measure the distances. The arrows shift your visual attention to cause you to assume that the center is more towards the right.

PERFECT FIT Does the width of the red figure (AB) equal the distance across the green (CD) or blue (EF) oval?

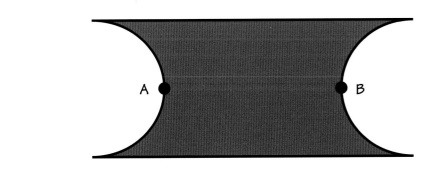

The length across the green oval (CD) is equal to the length across the red shape (AB). Those curved ends of CD make you think that it is shorter than it actually is. Although EF is longer than AB, it appears to be the same length as AB because its curved ends make it look shorter.

DECEITFUL DOTS Is the distance between the purple and orange spots the same as the distance between the orange and green spots?

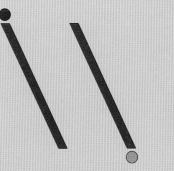

Although they don't look it, they are both the same lengths. Again, a wrong sense of 3-D processing is applied to the image. This causes your brain to overestimate the distance between the green and orange dots while underestimating the distance between the purple and orange dots.

Which of these three colored lines are the same length?

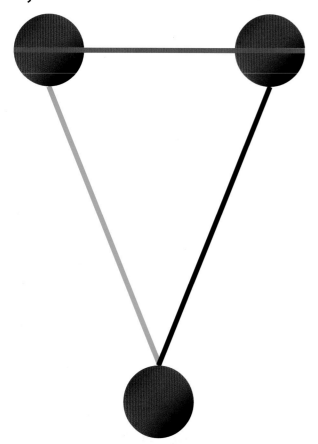

Would you believe all three lines are the same length? Sure, the green and black lines look similar in length, but the blue line is also the same length. It looks shorter because, unlike the other lines, this segment does not have the spheres providing the illusion of extended lengths. In addition, the enclosure of the blue line within the ends of the circles prematurely ends your concept of its length.

Are these lines parallel, or do alternate pairs come together and then spread apart?

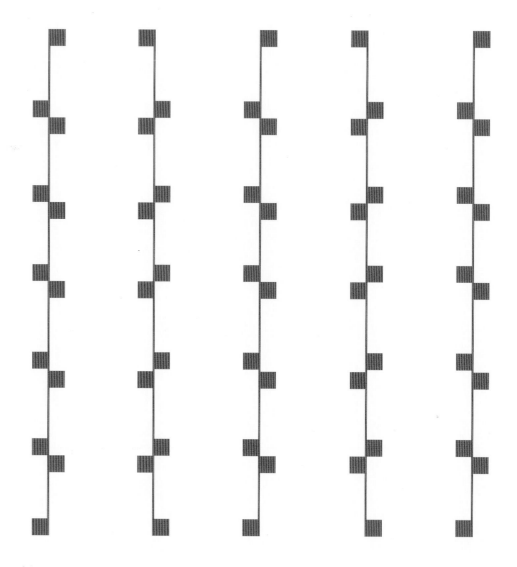

You may need a straightedge to check this out, but all of these lines are parallel. The offset squares trick your brain into creating imaginary tilts. These tilts produce the illusion of spreading and converging lines.

LLENGES

CAVE-IN How straight are the sides of this square? Are you sure?

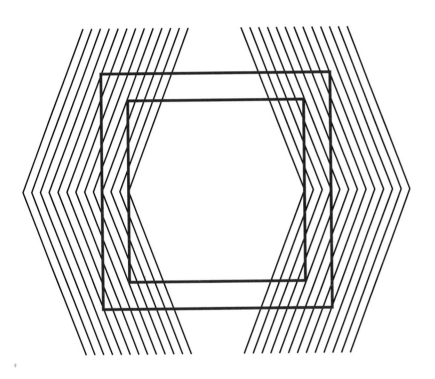

The sides are as straight as straight can be. It's that background pattern that confounds your brain. It produces a false sense of 3-D, complete with peaks and valleys. Once fooled, your brain applies its standard 3-D processing and creates a caved-in illusion.

Examine the column of horizontal lines. Are the top and bottom lines the same length?

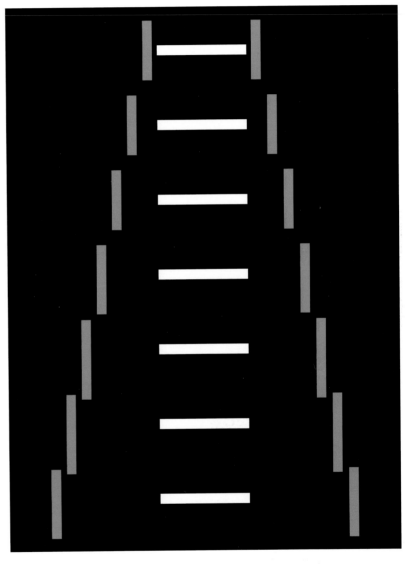

Yes, they are. Position a ruler along the edges of these horizontal lines and you'll discover that the lines are exactly the same length. The closed-in look of the top line tricks us into increasing this line's length. The open space at the bottom of the column suggests that these lines are smaller.

13

misguided Processing

So far you've seen how a misguided sense of 3-D processing can be used to explain some illusions. But how does this misguided thought proce[ss] work? We'll find out in these two pages.

SOME LIGHT READING

Light is a form of energy that streams through space. Created by objects such as stars (our sun), fires, and lightbulbs, light energy travels in straight lines that are often represented by rays.

When these rays enter our eyes, their image is cast upon a screen called the retina, which is at the back of the eye. The size of this cast image will depend upon two things: 1) the object's actual size; 2) the distance to the object.

The closer an object is to an observer, the larger the image that object will cast. The farther the object is, the smaller an image it will cast.

Close objects cast large images.

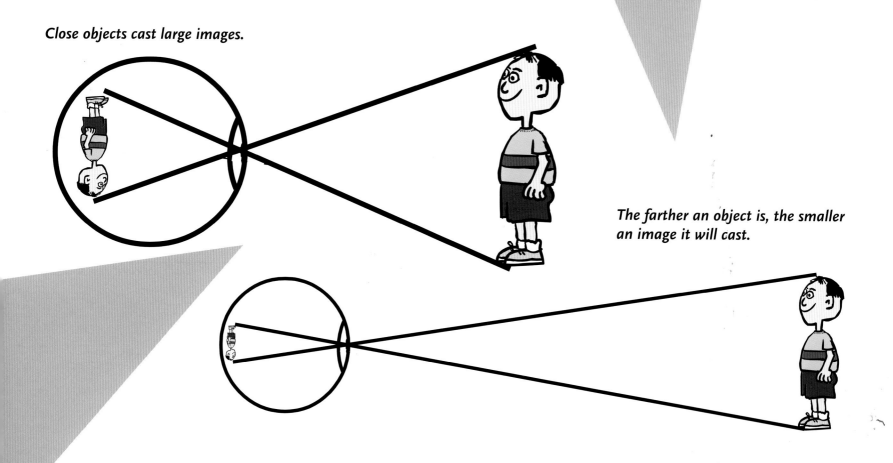

The farther an object is, the smaller an image it will cast.

RULE BOOKS

Our brains have built a rule book of consistency. When we see a tree in the distance, we know it is a full-sized tree. Without being aware of it, we use distance as a clue to "best guess" a reasonable size for this large object.

Suppose two same-sized images were cast upon our retina. One of the images comes from an object in the distance. The other comes from a nearby object. Since the images are the same size, but the assumed distance to the objects is different, our brain engages its 3-D processing.

"Ah-hah!" says the brain. "Since the images are the same size, the objects must be of different sizes (assuming one is close and the other is far away)." In order to cast the same-sized image, the farther object must be larger. Therefore, the brain performs an automatic stretch to the object and makes it appear bigger. Likewise, the nearby object remains small since it casts the same-sized image as the farther object.

INTO THE ILLUSION

Now that you know how the processing works, let's see step-by-step how it can be misguided.

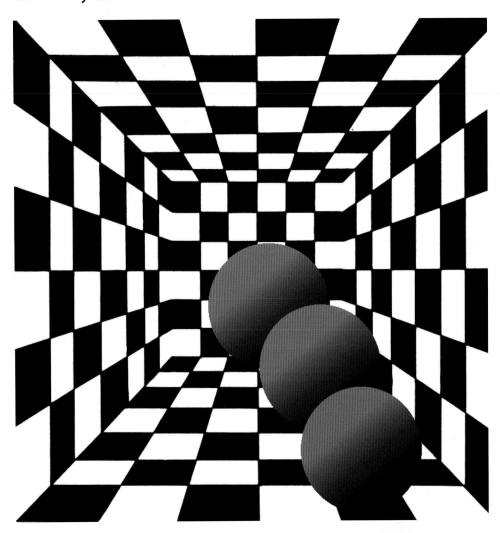

1. Your brain is tricked into thinking that this flat scene has depth.

2. The identical bowling balls cast same-sized images on your retina.

3. "Ah-hah!" says your tricked brain. Since the upper ball is farther away (because it is at the back of this 3-D hallway), it must be larger to produce this same-sized image.

4. The foolery is formed. Your brain "stretches" the image of the ball it falsely believes is farther away, making the two balls look different sizes.

Room for Mistakes

CLOCK CAPERS

Take a look at this clock. As you can see, it's far from being a perfect timepiece. It's been stretched out sideways.

Look from this direction

Now roll up a sheet of paper into a tube. Lay this page with the clock flat on a table. Close one eye and look down the tube. Tilt the tube to a sideways position in order to find the exact viewing angle so that the clock appears to be a perfect circle.

Once the clock appears circular, move the tube back so that you can also see the red dots. From this angle, do the red dots look the same size? Which red dot looks bigger?

The red dot closer to you looks bigger. That makes sense: things that are closer appear larger. The foolery, however, is getting your brain to accept that the two red dots are examined from the same distance. Since they appear to be the same viewing distance, one of the dots is logically larger than the other.

The dots, however, are the same size. Your brain can't tell because it was misled by the clock image. Once the clock looks like a circle, your brain guesses that the clock (and the whole page) is being viewed straight on even though it isn't. Since the entire scene is mistakenly thought to be of equal distance, any difference in red-dot size has to be attributed to a difference in the actual size of these dots.

AMES ROOM

Check out the two people in this room. What is happening? Obviously, some trickery is going on—but what?

This illusion is a more complex example of the clock image. Your brain is tricked into thinking that it is looking straight on at two people who are the same distance from the observer. But they aren't. The larger person is closer to you than the smaller person. The room's odd shape hides the true position of the two people. Since your brain didn't know that one is closer than the other, it attributes the difference in size to an actual difference in height.

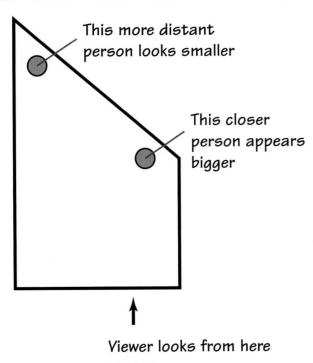

This more distant person looks smaller

This closer person appears bigger

↑

Viewer looks from here

A view of the Ames room shown from above.

TALL STUFF

Just think how adults look to toddlers. They must seem tall and towering. In fact, if you ever look at children's drawings, you'll see that they show adults as having very, very long legs. The extra leg length may seem exaggerated to us, but it's a pretty accurate view of what a child see when looking up.

TALL TALES

Here's an easy question: Is the dot placed halfway up the triangle? If not, how much is it off by?

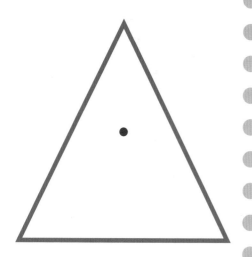

You may need a ruler to check this out, but that dot is exactly at the center. It appears, however, to be placed slightly higher than the midline.

Think about it. Is the trick caused by the tendency for things to appear "higher" than where they are placed, or is something else at work? Let's flip the triangle over and see if the dot still appears to rise above the center.

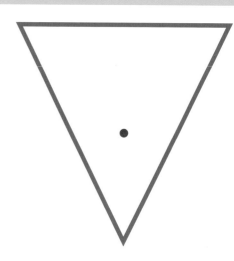

Now it seems to be lower than the center. So our theory that "things seem to rise higher" isn't correct. What happens when we flip the figure to either side?

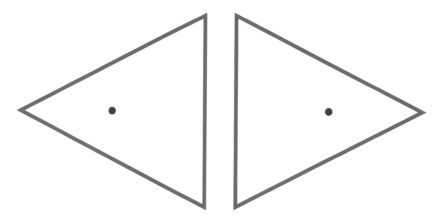

The dot still appears to be closer to the nearby angle than the far side of the triangle. Although no one is certain why this is so, one explanation suggests that open and closed spaces affect the way we see an object. The dot appears closer to the "walled in" area of the angle than the open space of the distant side. That's only one theory. What's yours?

HATS OFF TO ABE

President Abraham Lincoln was a tall man. By adding on a stovepipe hat he appeared even taller. But did you know that by itself a stovepipe hat can act as an illusion? Look at this hat. Is the hat taller than the brim is wide?

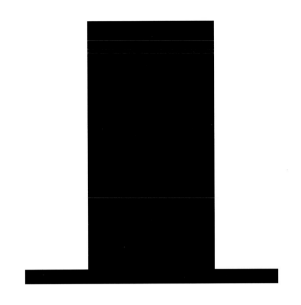

They're the same length. Yet most people see that the hat is slightly taller than the brim is wide. Often, we see vertical lines longer than horizontal lines of the same length.

This illusion may also arise from how we see interrupted lines. The horizontal brim is cut by the bowl of the hat. This makes the brim appear chopped and shorter. Since the stovepipe bowl is not crossed along its length, it retains its original, lengthy appearance.

EQUAL STACK
Examine the three stacks below. One stack has a height (measured from upper edge A to lower edge B) equal to its width. Which one is it?

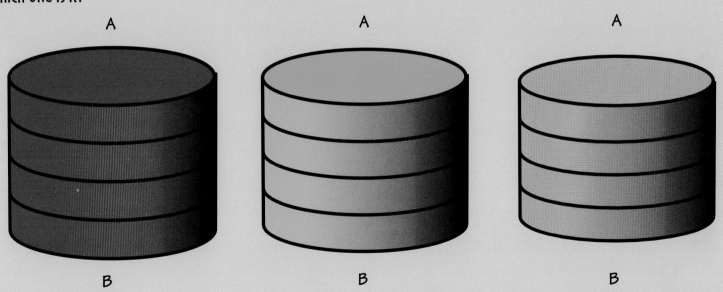

The first stack has the equal dimensions. It probably doesn't appear that way because several optical tricks are at work. The first twist is that we ordinarily tend to stretch objects to make them appear somewhat taller than what they actually are. The second twist has to do with the 3-D appearance of the stacks. This extra processing further confuses your perception. The third has to do with the extra length we tack onto the stacks because of the printed letters.

SHIFTING ATTENTION

FRASER'S SPIRAL What's in a name? Everything? Nothing? Take a look at the figure below. It's called Fraser's spiral, and this effect was first created back in 1908. Notice anything odd about Mr. Fraser's spiral? How about the fact that it's not a spiral?

That's right, Fraser's spiral is not a spiral. It's a set of concentric circles. Your perception of this image, however, gets twisted so that the circles appear to spiral inwards.

Different tricks are at work here. First, the circles are not drawn as solid lines. Instead, they are formed from what appears to be a twisted cord. Second, most people will agree that the background produces a strong feeling of motion. This may cause your eye's attention to spin inwards, taking your focus along the gentle twists of a spiral. As a result, your brain thinks that if your visual attention spins like a spiral, then it must be a spiral.

TWISTED OUTLOOK

You don't need curved lines to twist an appearance. Notice how this pattern of triangles tricks your brain into seeing slightly slanted walls.

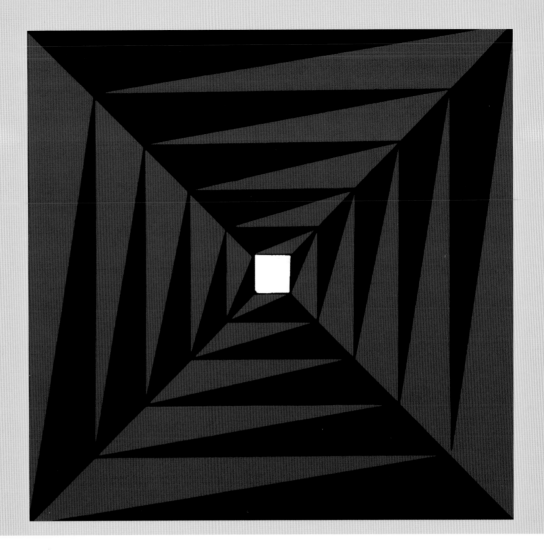

SHIFTY EYES

Patterns and shapes that surround an object can create all sorts of effects. As you've seen, twists and turns can produce a spiral when there is no spiral. They can also change the way a person appears.

Take a look at these two people. Which one is looking at you? Which isn't? Are you sure?

Both of them are looking at the same place. Their eyes are identical!

If you don't believe it, just cover up everything except the eyes and you'll see that their gaze is the same. It's the other cues, such as shadows and face angles, that affect how we perceive the direction of their gaze.

CREATURE FEATURE

1. Photocopy the creature shown on the opposite page onto heavy-stock paper.

2. Use a pair of scissors to carefully cut out the two circular eye-holes in the creature's face.

3. Use your scissors to punch a slit on either side of the eye-holes where shown.

4. Photocopy or trace the eye insert shown below.

5. Use your scissors to cut out this insert.

NOTE: Make sure that you don't cut off the two small tabs that extend from both ends of this band.

6. Slightly arch the eye insert and tuck its tabs into the face slits. Make sure that the printed eyes face into the mask.

7. Use tape to secure the tabs.

8. Hold the creature upright. You can prop it up against a book.

9. Stand back. Observe the watchful stare of the creature's eyes.

Side view

Top view

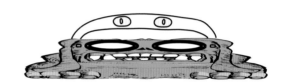

What happens to the creature's gaze when you move to either side?

CAUTION: If necessary, have an adult help you cut out the different parts and make the slits for the creature.

As you move your head from side to side, the watchful eyes seem to follow you. This effect arises from the eyeballs being in a different plane than the eye cutouts. As you shift your position, you get a different vantage through the mask holes. The change in viewing angle places the eyeballs in a different spot within the cutout. Your brain attempts to make sense of this by creating a scene in which the eyeballs acquire a smooth, side-to-side movement.

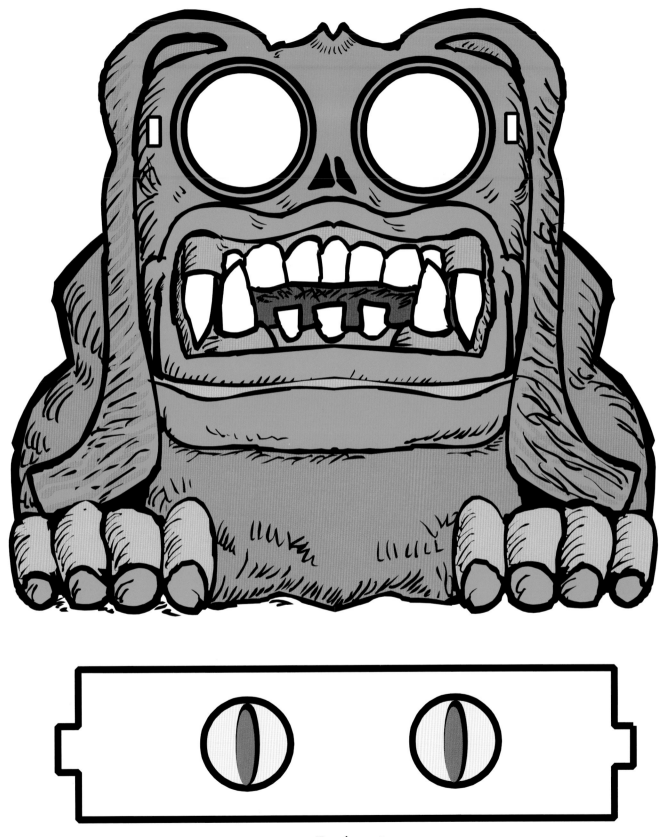

Eye insert

Illusions in Print

Look right here. What do you see? Most likely, you "visualize" printed words on a page in an optical illusion book. Good.

But where is the image of this page really located? Is the image out here in 3-D space? Can you grasp and handle the visualization? Or is an image located somewhere else? We'll find out on these two pages.

WHAT'S YOUR SIGN? Read this sign quickly!

**STOP!
READ THIS
Optical Illusion Magic is a
a fun book filled with all
sorts of visual tricks and
and mind-boggling
images.
THE END.**

Is there anything wrong with this sign? You bet there is! Reread it. Did you find the mistakes?

When we read, we focus on the content of the sentence. Words like "a" and "and" may be skipped over since they are not critical to the whole meaning of the sentence. As you quickly read this sentence, your focus jumped from the terms "Optical Illusion Magic" to "fun book" to "visual tricks." In doing so, you overlooked the double printing of less significant words.

A QUICK COUNT Count the number of times the letter "f" appears in the following paragraph:

All forms of optical illusions seem to fascinate folks. In fact, my favorite friends find visual foolery fantastically fun, if not incredibly fascinating. But suppose such folks found illusions foolish and flat? If that were a fact, then books of this style might be defunct.

How many did you count? Was it twenty-one? Although you probably spotted the "f" in large words, you might have overlooked the "f" in shorter words, such as "of" and "if."

FLIPPED OUT Quickly look at the line of letters below. Which color of letters appear more symmetrical? Make a choice, then spin this page upside down and look again.

S S S S S S S

To most of us, the black S appears more symmetrical. The key word is "appears." Both the purple and black letters are the same, but the purple letters are upside down.

We have gotten used to seeing an asymmetrical (bottom heavy) S and accept it as its normal appearance. However, when the S is flipped upside down, the imbalance becomes very noticeable and we quickly identify the S's with a small bottom curve.

EIGHTS OR BETTER?

Which of these numbers appears more symmetrical? Make a choice, then spin this page upside down and look again.

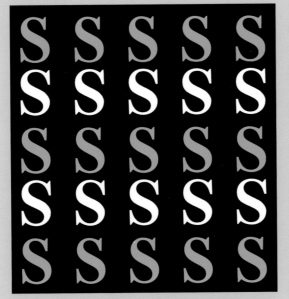

Again, we are familiar with the "bottom-heavy" appearance of the number 8. It's more easily accepted and so it doesn't seem as an imbalanced symbol to us.

IMBALANCED BALANCE?

Do the white letters appear "top heavy"?

They're not. We get used to seeing an S with a slightly smaller top half. Therefore, when an S with two equal halves is presented, it appears asymmetrical.

GRAY AREA

Even the photographic images in newspapers are illusions. Use a magnifying lens and you'll see that regions that appear as shades of gray are actually made up of varying sizes of black ink dots.

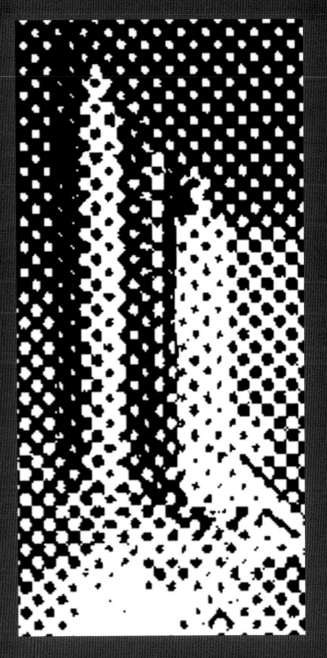

WHAT'S MY LINE?

Which line is longer, the red or the green?

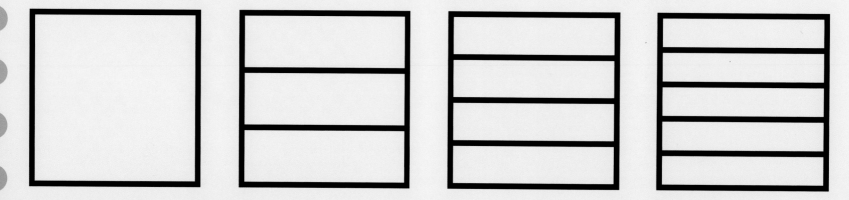

Would you believe that the green line is longer than the red? Use a ruler and you'll uncover a powerful visual trick. Your brain gets tricked by several misleading cues. One cue is the stretching that is wrongfully applied to the segment with filled squares that extend the ends. Another misleading cue comes from isolating the green segment within a long length of line. This isolation makes the line look smaller than it actually is.

FILL 'ER UP Which square appears tallest?

The square with the most lines probably appears tallest. Although all four squares are the same size, the "fill" tricks your brain into overestimating the dimensions.

26

LINEAGE OF FOOLERY Which length is longer, AB or BC?

BC is actually longer than AB. Check it out with a ruler and you'll see how filling an area with lines tricks your brain into thinking that the area is longer than it actually is.

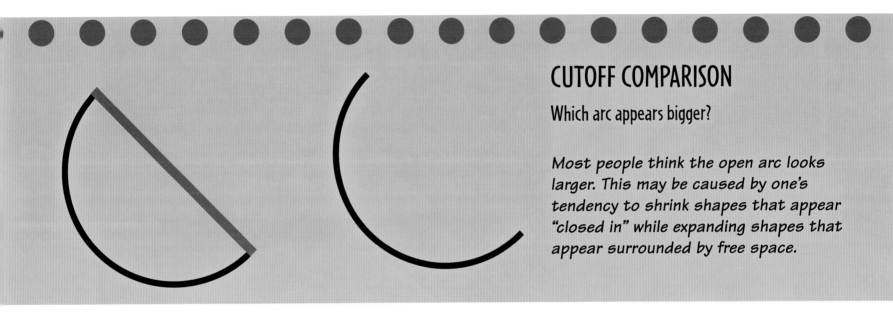

CUTOFF COMPARISON

Which arc appears bigger?

Most people think the open arc looks larger. This may be caused by one's tendency to shrink shapes that appear "closed in" while expanding shapes that appear surrounded by free space.

ALLEY ARTIFACT

Which length is longer, AB or BC?

As you may have guessed, these lengths are the same. The partial squares produce an illusion of greater area than the same-sized region located between the two green lines. This causes your brain to underestimate the inner distance, producing this illusionary effect.

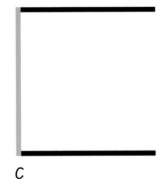

A   B   C

Standing Out

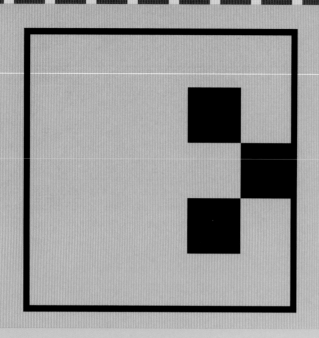

Process. Process. Process. Our visual system is constantly at work trying to make sense out of the images our eyes detect.

Take a look at this pattern of three blocks. What do you see?

HINT: Give your visual processing system some time to figure it out.

Do you see the letter E? Although it might be difficult to see the E at first, you'll have no problem in finding it now that you know what to expect. This pattern has been recorded into your visual experience and processing record book.

POP GOES THE FIGURE

What's in this image?

1. Four white hour glasses

2. Small black four-blade pinwheel

3. Larger white four-blade pinwheel

Any and all of the shapes mentioned can be found in this image. It depends upon what parts of the background you "pop" into the foreground.

CLUTTER

Have you ever searched a messy room looking for a missing toy? Finally, just as you are about to give up, the toy appears right in plain sight. Although it was there all this time, the toy was hidden by clutter. Your eyes detect its shape, but your brain doesn't assemble a clear view of the scene.

Now here's another hidden view that's in plain sight. Can you identify the subject of this splattered picture?

It's a Dalmatian curled up on the ground. Its nose is off to the right. Its curled tail is on the left.

CATCHING Z'S

This pattern is formed by rows of Z's that are tilted in three different directions. Can you uncover all three tilts? Can you see all three tilts at once or must you "switch" from one slope to another?

Most people will see only one, or perhaps two, of the slopes very quickly, but they will have a difficult time seeing the third slope. Once they do, people have to switch "attention gears" in order to see each of the three slopes. Most people will not see all three at the same time.

PROBLEMATIC PATTERNS

Would you believe that these stacks of square blocks are perfectly vertical?

The pattern may be too much for your brain to handle. As your brain begins to organize the units into vertical columns, it assigns a "slant" to its processing. This produces the appearance of stacks that appear slightly crooked.

ORGANIZE, ORGANIZE, ORGANIZE

At close range, you can see that this pattern is made up of circles. But what happens to these circles when you hold the page at a distance?

Two changes in appearance occur. First, you organize this featureless pattern into familiar shapes, such as triangles, hexagons, rows, columns, and slanted lines. Second, the circles change their shape into six-sided figures called hexagons.

FAST FLOWER FIND How fast can you uncover the flower that is missing a single petal?

Even though there were three hundred flowers, you spotted the odd image within seconds! This ability to uncover things that stick out is wired into your visual processing ability.

HIGHS AND LOWS OF LIGHT

Does this pattern of rings appear to open towards the upper left or lower right?

Most people will first see the rings as pointing towards the upper left. But keep looking at the center. The appearance will soon flip towards the lower right.

The image is drawn so that it can be viewed either way. However, lighting cues suggest that the rings pointing towards the upper left are more logical than the rings pointing to the lower right.

Most of the time light comes to us from above through such sources as the sun, ceiling fixtures, and streetlights. Because we are used to that, we interpret scenes using this lighting angle.

If we imagine that a light is placed above our 3-D ring pattern, it must be located to the upper right. Therefore, the rings appear to open to the upper left. Since this is a logical position for a light, we have a tendency to interpret the image in this orientation.

A less logical position for a light source is to have it come up from the lower right. Only after we look at this image for several seconds will this alternate orientation emerge.

Logical light direction

Appears to open this way

Appears to open this way

Less logical light direction

BOXED IN BY THE LIGHT Describe this shape.

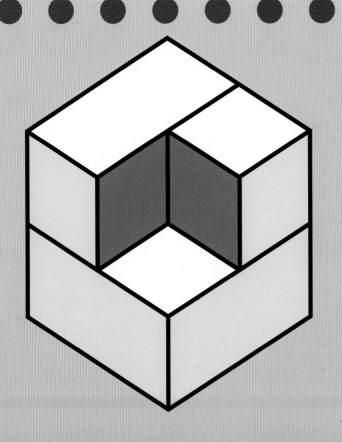

This is another image that can present two logical appearances. What it looks like depends on the direction you assign to the light source. If the light comes from above, the image looks like a simple cube that has its top corner missing. If, however, you assume that the light comes from below, it appears to be a small box that is positioned in the corner of a ceiling.

33

TALLER OF TWO Which shape appears taller?

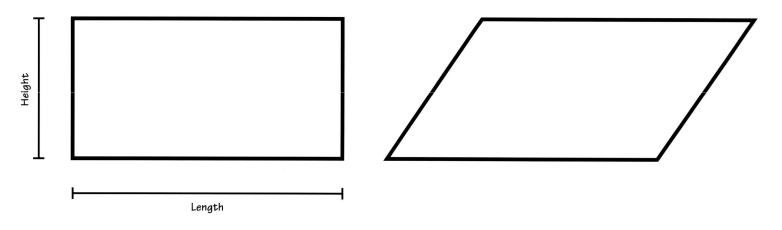

The rectangle and the slanted rectangle (or parallelogram) are the exact same height. Measure them with a ruler and you'll discover that they're also the same width. The slanted appearance tricks us into overestimating the dimensions and areas of shapes.

FULL-FILLED POTENTIAL   Suppose we filled the shapes? Does the parallelogram still appear to have greater dimensions than the rectangle?

You bet it does. This illusion has nothing to do with fill. Its effect is based solely upon the slanted sides.

FILL 'ER UP Let's keep experimenting with this illusion. How do various fill patterns affect the illusion? You be the judge.

When the fill pattern contains parallel lines, the illusion of greater dimension still exists.

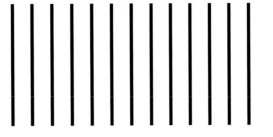 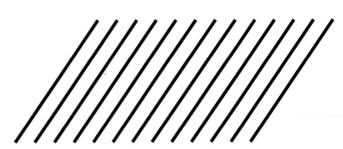

What about now?

The illusion loses much of its effect. Although the parallelogram may appear bigger, the perceived difference is reduced. The slanted lines that fill the rectangle seem to make the rectangle appear closer in the size to the parallelogram.

How about now?

When both shapes are filled with a pattern of slanted lines, the illusion appears to lose most, if not all, of its effect.

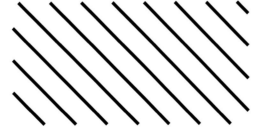 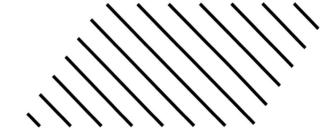

BUILDING ILLUSIONS

Did you know that the ancient Greeks used optical illusions to improve the appearance of their temples? Without the help of these visual tricks, the temples would appear less magnificent.

Can you match the building trick with the effect it was meant to correct?

1. The floor and roof curve upwards in the middle.

2. The columns have a "thickened" midsection.

3. The tops of pillars are tilted back into the temple.

a. Standing in front of a temple, columns appear to tilt outwards from the strucuture.

b. Standing in front of a temple, a straight roof and floor appear to sag in the middle.

c. An upright cylinder appears thicker at the ends than in its middle.

Answer: 1-b, 2-c, 3-a.

PERFECTLY PROBLEMATIC PILLARS

Speaking of columns, do you notice any problems with these?

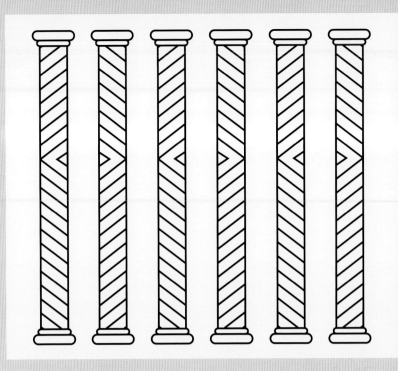

These columns are perfectly straight, vertical, and parallel to each other. The slanted lines drawn in the columns create a false sense of 3-D. Your misguided visual processing goes to work and "repaints" the scene as a set of bent columns.

NORTHERN EXPOSURE
Here's a better challenge. Which is longer, the red line or the green line?

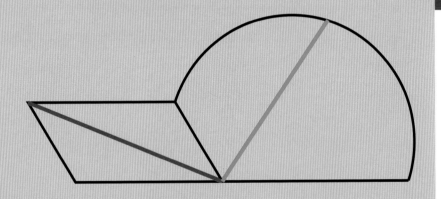

HINT: Try imagining the red and green lines as sides of a rectangle. When you get the orientation, it's easier to see the red line as being slightly longer.

At first glance, the lines may look the same length. However, if you use a ruler you'll discover that the red line is longer. The curved shape tricks your mind into stretching the appearance of the green line. So although they are not the same length, they look like they are.

BUILDING AN EXTENSION
Imagine extending the orange line towards the blue line. Would it meet up with the endpoint of the blue line or would it cross the blue line at another point along its length?

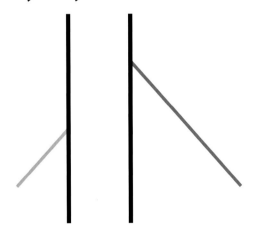

If extended, the orange line will meet at the exact endpoint of the blue line. The angles formed by intersecting lines cause your focus to stray downward and make you incorrectly think that the lines will not meet at the endpoints.

37

HOT STUFF

Have you ever seen a picture in which the colors clash so much that they appear to be moving? Take a look at this blob of red. Gently move the page back and forth in a swirling motion. Does the blob remain the same or does it look wobbly?

HOLY SPOKES! Hold this page upright and spin it in small, tight circles. Don't spin it too fast. Keep looking at the center of this pattern. Do you see the illusionary spiral spokes that appear to race around the circles? How does the direction of the spoke movement compare with the direction of the book spin?

Your vision has a hard time adjusting to colors that clash, especially when they are on top of each other. Since it is difficult to keep track of this clashing edge where they meet, your visual processing accepts it as a soft and changeable outline. That's why this blob wobbles.

No one knows for certain why we see these spokes, but some psychologists believe it has to do with confused communication between the cells in our eyes.

VIBRATING VISUALS Back in the 1960s, Op Art was very popular. This illustration style used highly contrasting shapes and patterns to produce a sensation of movement called visual vibration. Look into this figure and you'll see that many of the edges appear to have an "electric" or glowing quality.

MOON ILLUSION

Close your eyes and think of the moon. First imagine the moon somewhere high above in the nighttime sky. Now think of the moon positioned at the horizon. In which spot does the moon seem larger?

Most people will say that the moon appears much bigger at the horizon. But why? Is this an illusion made up in your mind? Or is there something physical in this change of appearance? Of the four choices below, what do you think is the correct answer?

a. The moon gets magnified by distorted light rays.

b. At the horizon, the moon is compared to nearby objects, not stars.

c. The angle that your head tilts back to see the moon affects how your brain approximates its size.

d. Scientists still don't know why we see this illusion.

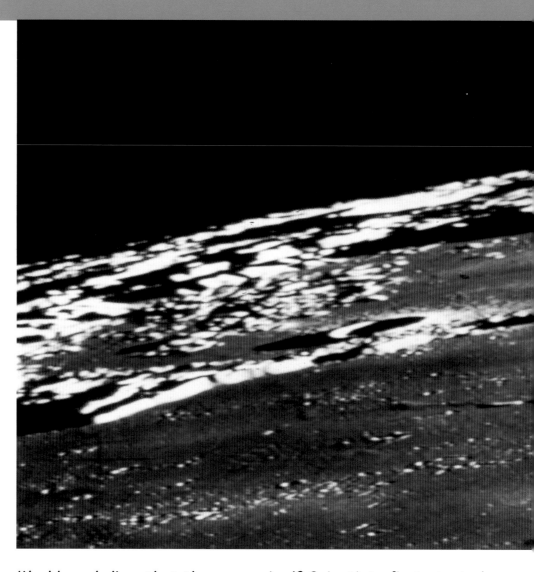

Would you believe that the answer is d? Scientists first started studying the moon illusion about 2500 years ago. Although there are all sorts of proposed theories, they still aren't certain why we see this illusion.

WHAT'S YOUR GUESS? How large is the moon? Suppose you hold a dime at arm's length. Can this coin block out the entire moon or will it cover only a part of it?

Surprisingly, the dime is larger than the moon. Held at an arms distance, the dime will completely block it out. Most people are surprised to discover that a small dime can do this. They have a preconception that the moon fills much more of the nighttime sky than it actually does.

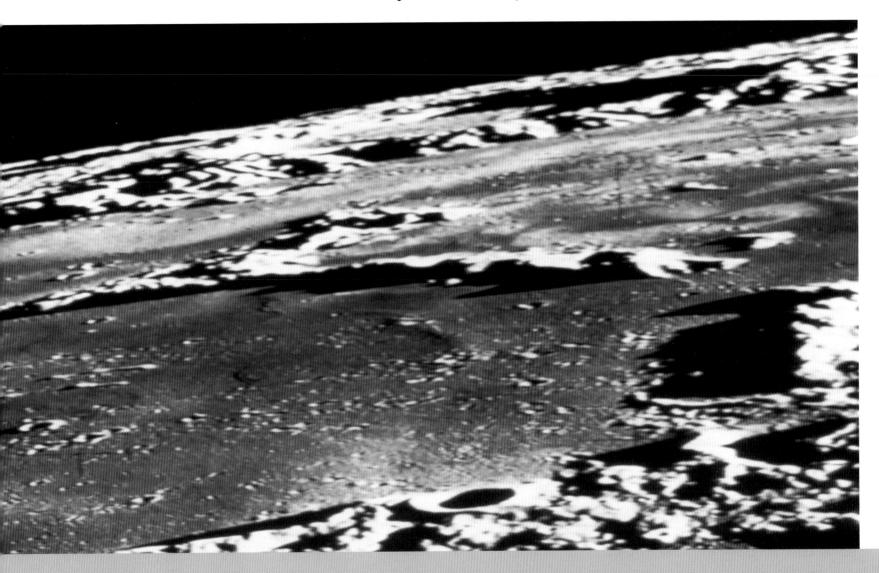

MORE MOON MADNESS On a partly cloudy night, look at the moon. As the clouds pass the moon in one direction, the moon seems to move in the opposite direction. This is an illusion of apparent motion. But there's more. Even though the moon seems to be moving, it also seems to be in the same spot. How can the moon be moving and yet at the same spot? Strange, but true, your brain accepts two conflicting views of what you see!

Many people say that the moon looks closer when it is at the horizon. Therefore, it appears larger. What do you think? Does the horizon moon appear to be consistent in its size to the overhead moon, but seem closer to Earth? Or do you think that the moon appears the same distance at the horizon, but is different in size?

RISE AND SINK

A pattern can be much more than a design that fills or adds color to an object. When used correctly, patterns can create a 3-D illusion. Just look at the examples on these two pages.

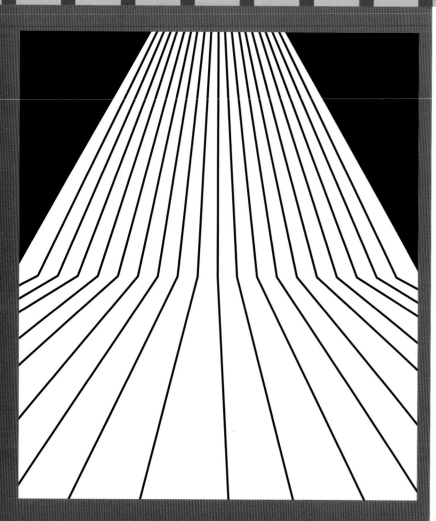

The pattern of angles in this illustration gives the illusion of depth.

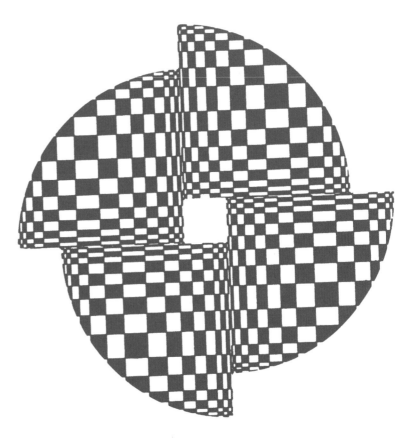

This "sliced" circle has a 3-D appearance created by the checkerboard pattern. Notice how the shape seems to drop or bend in regions that have compressed checkerboard squares.

Take a look at this thick line with two bumps. By itself, it creates a slight feeling of depth. But once it is repeated in a pattern, its 3-D effect intensifies.

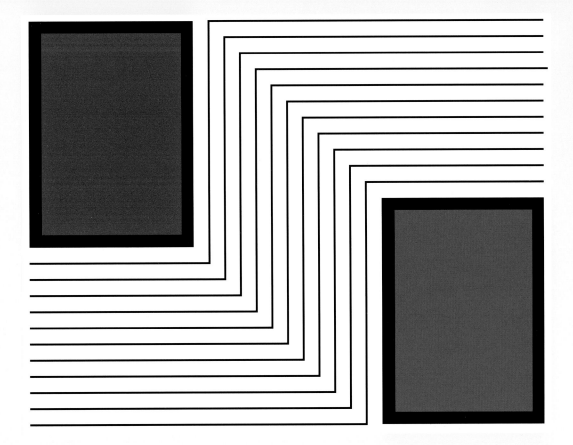

The red or blue box can seem to be on top of the stack. Can you switch their positions in your mind?

Shady Comparisons

STRIPE ONE Take a look at the blue stripes in each of the two circles. Are they the same shade of blue or is one darker than the other?

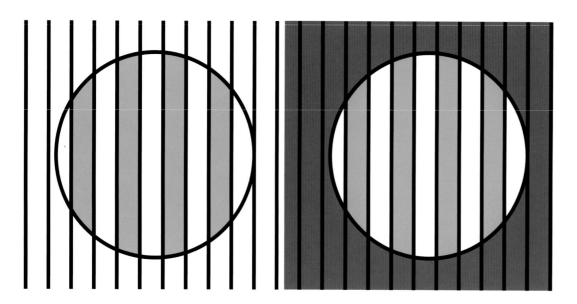

Although they don't appear it, the stripes in each of the circles are the exact same shade. It's the blue background behind the second circle that sends your brain on to a faulty shortcut. Against this darker surrounding, the inner stripes of the second circle look brighter and so your brain retains this concept of "bright" when it compares the shades of the stripes.

PURPLE SQUARES

These two purple squares are:

a. The exact same size (only one is rotated on its side)

b. The same shade of purple

c. Slightly different sizes

d. Slightly different shades of purple

e. Both a and b

f. Both c and d

Believe it or not, the correct answer is e—both purple squares are the exact same shade and size. The different shades of gray create an unfair comparison background. Your brain incorrectly processes the purple surrounded by the darker background as a light shade. In addition, the rotated appearance of a square makes it appear larger.

RING

Take a close look at this ring. Is the top half the same thickness as the bottom half? Or is the bottom half slightly thicker? Is the shade the same around the entire ring or is half of it printed in a slightly different shade?

The top and bottom halves of the ring are the same thickness. Use a ruler and you'll discover that their width is the same. In addition, the ring is printed in the same shade throughout its length.

Two illusions are at work here. The distortions in size and shading are produced by the background patterns. These patterns lead your visual processing astray and suggest a false sense of 3-D. They also offer an inconsistent background for comparison.

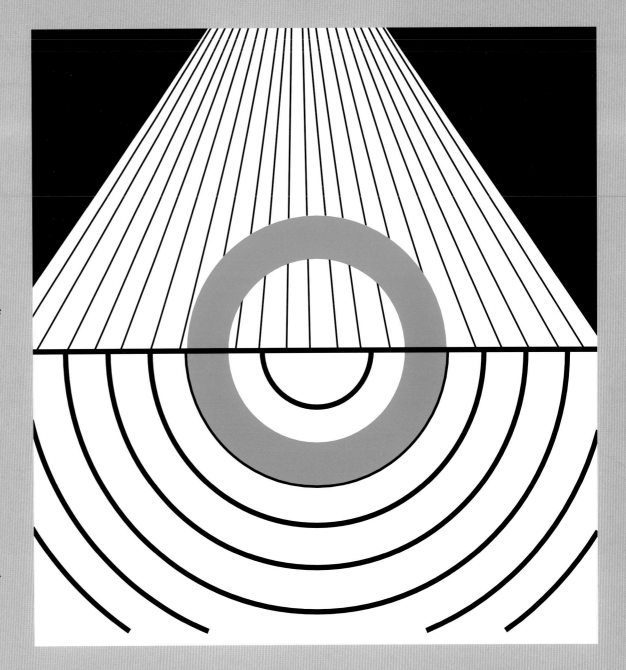

A PRIMER ON PRIMARY COLORS

When light rays strike an object, some of the rays are reflected. These reflected rays carry the "image" of an object. When the rays enter our eye, they are detected and start a chain of events that finishes with our mind's-eye view of the outside world.

RED, ORANGE, YELLOW, GREEN, BLUE, VIOLET

Each color has a distinct, wavelike shape.

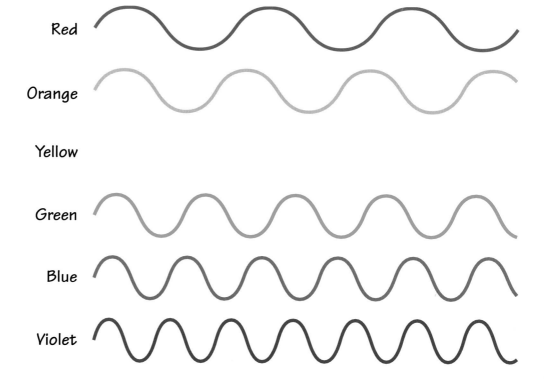

Red

Orange

Yellow

Green

Blue

Violet

WHITE

White is not a color of light. It is what we "see" when a mixture of colors is detected by our eyes. Instead of seeing distinct colors, our brain interprets this as the sensation of white.

When all colors are reflected off an object, we detect white.

BLACK

Like white, black is not a color of light. Black is the sensation we get when our eyes do not detect any light.

When all colors are absorbed by an object, we detect black.

When all colors except for red are absorbed, we see red.

ADD OR SUBTRACT?

Have you ever mixed colors of paint? If so, you know that by mixing the right colors you can produce a limitless assortment of shades. As different pigments are added to the mixture, they absorb certain colors, which takes away from the total light reflected off the paint. This "taking away" process is called subtractive mixing of colors.

Mixing colored lights is a completely different story. When colored lights are shown on the same spot, no colors are taken away. In fact, as different colors of light are added, the amount of reflected light increases. This process is known as additive mixing of colors.

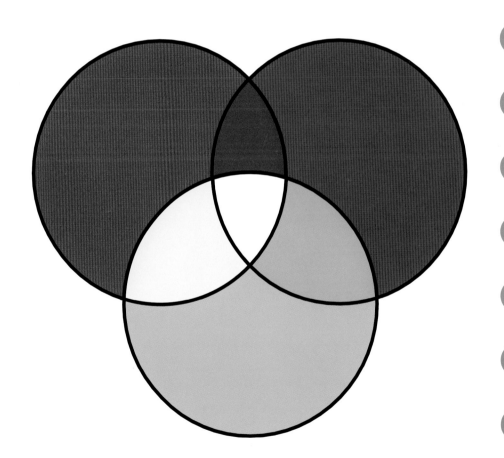

Here's what happens when red, green, and blue lights are mixed together. The additive properties combine to form more colors.

COLOR TRICKS

Think of an apple. What color is it? Most of you would think of a red apple. But this apple doesn't absorb red light. It mostly reflects red. Since red light bounces off the apple's surface, this is the color that our eyes detect. Other colors, such as blue, yellow, and purple, are mostly absorbed by the apple. As a result, they never reach our eyes.

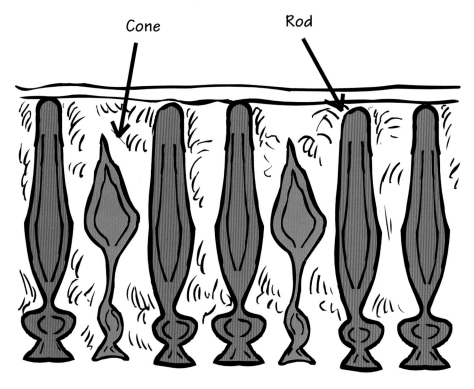

Cone　　　　Rod

OF RODS AND CONES

Your eye has two types of specialized cell that can detect light: rods and cones. Rods cannot detect color. They interpret the world in shades of gray. But rods work very well in dim light.

Cones, however, can detect colors. But, unlike rods, cones cannot function in low-light situations. In order to see colors, your eyes must be stimulated by brighter scenes.

THREE FLAVORS OF CONES

Your eyes have three types of color-detecting cone: red, green, and blue (violet). Each type of cone detects only a single color.

When they work together, the three kinds of cone can pick up millions of different colors. By analyzing the response from the three types of cone, your brain creates any color in the rainbow. For example, when green and red cones send the right mix of signals to the brain, we "see" yellow.

COLORS ON THE SPIN

To explore the additive color effects of this spinner, you'll need:

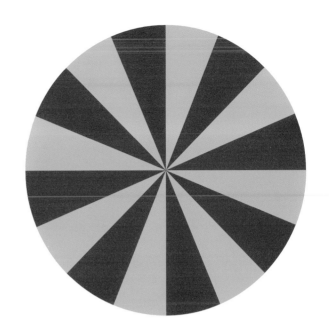

Scissors
Color photocopy/printout or hand-drawn copy of this pattern
Large paper clip
Pushpin
Green and red crayons and ruler (if you're drawing the disk)

STEPS

1. Make a color photocopy of this disk on a sheet of heavy-stock paper. If you can't make a photocopy, you can trace this pattern and fill in the sectors with green and red crayons.

2. Use your scissors to cut out this disk.

3. Use a pushpin to punch a hole through the center of the disk.

CAUTION: Have an adult punch the hole if you need help.

4. Bend a large paper clip into this shape.

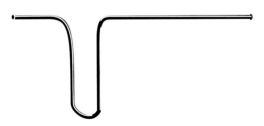

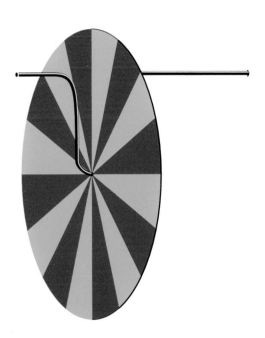

5. Insert the paper clip through the disk hole. The disk should be supported in the center of the bend and remain upright.

6. Begin spinning the disk as fast as you can. Look at the whirling mix of colors. What do you see?

As the wheel spins, both the red and green colors are cast upon your retina. Your brain tries to interpret this mix of signals according to its master cookbook of color composition. If the balance is right, this spinning mix produces the exact same signal as pure yellow.

49

STAND

As you've seen in the previous pages, you can produce a new color by viewing a rapidly changing pattern. There is another method to create colors without using a spinning wheel. It is based upon your limitation in focus.

DOT DILEMMA

Take a look at the patterns shown on these two pages. You probably have very little difficulty in identifying the colors printed here. Now prop up this book so this spread remains open. Walk to the far side of the room. Don't look at the book while you're moving. At the opposite end of the room, look at these patterns again. What do you see?

The image takes on a yellow cast! At a distance, the red and green dots are no longer distinct. Their light blends together. The red cones and green cones react to the light. Because they can't focus on the individual dots, they see the entire image as a blur and your brain processes the mixture of color as yellow.

MAKE A GUESS

What color do you think this pattern of blue and yellow dots will appear when viewed from across the room?

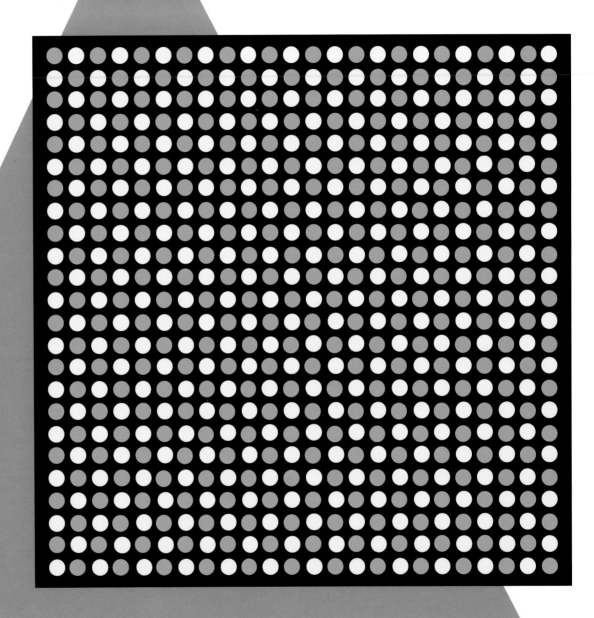

The image takes on a green cast.

FOUR-COLOR RAINBOW

Red. Blue. Yellow. Black. If you examine the ink cartridge of a desktop printer, you'll discover that these devices use only these four colors of ink. Yet they can print out millions of different shades.

Take a close look at the image on the right. Use a hand lens to magnify the print. What do you see?

Here's a magnified section of this printed image.

The printed image is made up of a pattern of four-color dots. Your brain averages this mixture of colors to produce a smooth and continuous rainbow of colors.

DUCKS IN THE PARK

Look closely into this image and you'll see that the shapes are not painted with strokes of the brush. Instead, they are created solely by dots. This style, known as Pointillism, uses points of paint on a surface so that, from a distance, they blend together. It was made famous in the 1800s by the French artist Georges Seurat.

DISCO SPIN

You don't need all the colors of the rainbow to see "white." In fact, your visual system will see white using only three colors.

COLORS INTO WHITE

As you can see, this disk is a mix of red, green, and blue. Follow the instructions on page 49 to construct a disk spinner. Can you get this whirling pattern to produce the illusion of white?

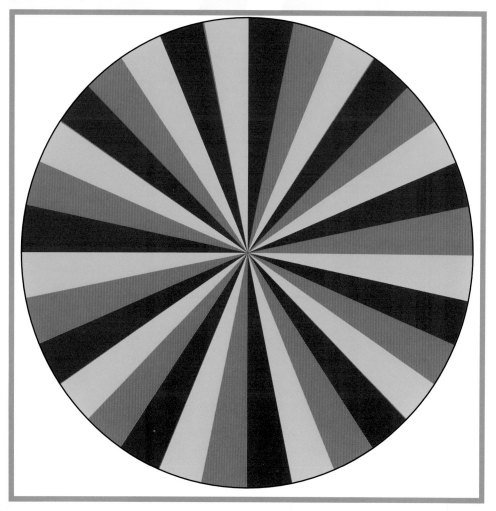

WHERE'S WHITE WHITE?

As these colors spin, you many not see pure white. In order to see pure white, you need an incredible balance of several factors. These include the correct color (hue and saturation) and the right spin speed. It also depends on the brightness of the room. Your three-color cones respond differently at different levels of light. Therefore, one disk cannot work in all situations.

So if you don't see white, try brightening or dimming the room. You can also try making up your own color combinations and seeing if you can produce a better color-blending disk!

READY TO RELOAD

As you've seen so far, not all cones are created equal. Some detect only green. Others see only blue. And still others only react to red. But there are other differences between these three cone types.

After a cone sends a nerve signal, it needs time to "reload." Although this "preparing to react" takes only a fraction of a second, it is a critical time during which a cone can't respond to light.

Some cones reload quicker than others. This means that after sending signals, one color of cone is ready to send again while the other cones are still reloading. So when a white target is displayed, only the cones that are ready to react will respond to this stimulus. This produces an unbalanced response that leads your brain into "seeing" colors that don't exist. Want to see?

COLORS FROM NOWHERE

Do you want to see colors where there are no colors? Then build this interesting spinner. Follow the instructions on page 49 if you've forgotten how.

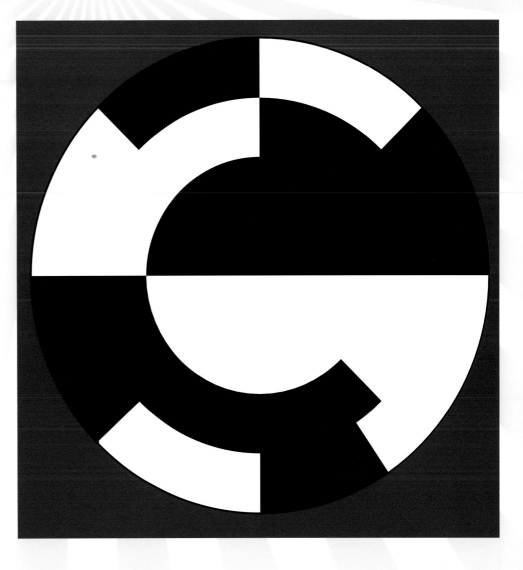

Although all psychologists can't agree on why this effect occurs, most of them believe that it involves the difference in the reloading times of the cones.

As the disk spins, the white regions stimulate the red, green, and blue cones. When the black spins into view, the cones reload before they send again. Since some of the cones reload quicker than others, not all cones react to the white. This produces an unbalanced response, which is decoded and processed by the brain into an imaginary color.

WEIRD SPINNERS

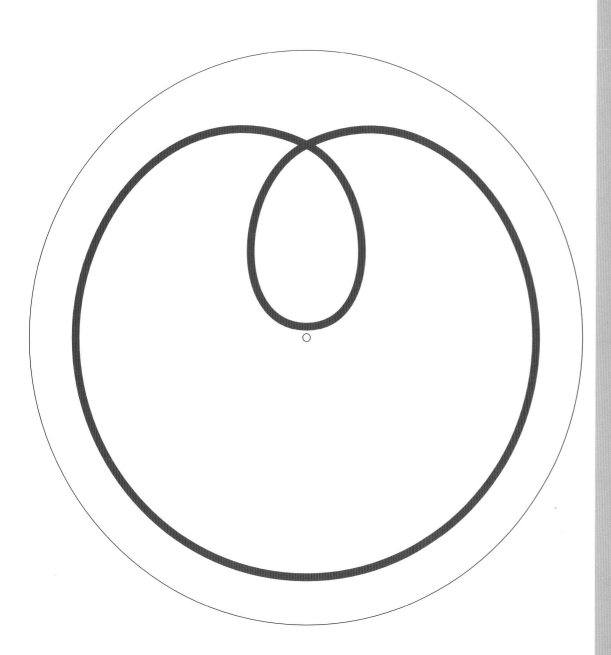

Not all spinning illusions produce color effects. Some trick your brain into twisting and distorting shapes because your brain can't get a stationary handle on the image.

DISTORTED CURVES

Copy this pattern onto a sheet of paper. Use a pair of scissors to cut it out. Poke a hole through the center circle and place the disk on a lazy Susan. Spin the rotating plate moderately and steadily.

BRAIN TWIST

Here's another weird spinner that creates the illusion of lines that twist and bend. To see this effect, all you have to do is rotate the book. For its strongest effect, photocopy this shape onto a sheet of paper. Cut it out and punch a hole in its center. Place this on a lazy Susan. Spin and watch the never-ending twists.

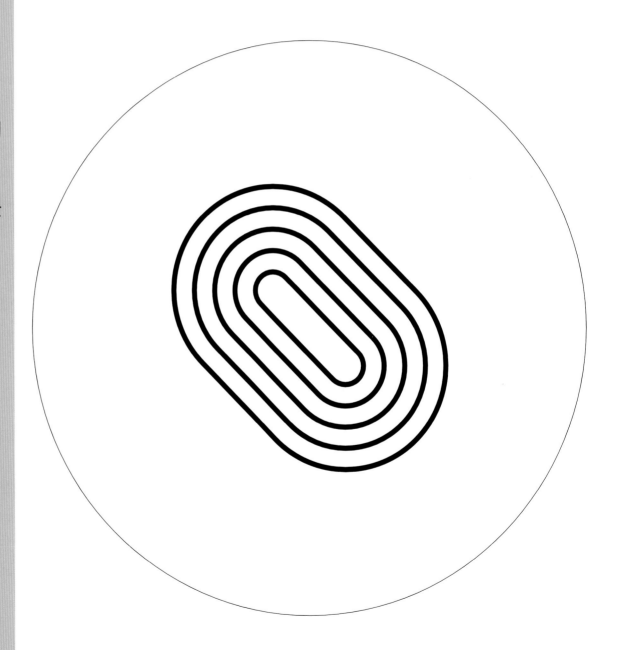

TRAILING BEHIND

Quickly wave your hand in front of you. What do you see? The movement creates a blurry trail of a moving hand. The blur is caused by your brain's tendency to hang onto an image. Scientists refer to this staying power as persistence of vision.

FLIPBOOKS

Flipbooks are a simple and fun way to create the illusion of motion. When you quickly flip through its pages, your brain becomes overloaded with information from the book's images. Because of persistence of vision, you get an image that appears to move with the illusion of smooth and uninterrupted motion.

BUILD THIS BOOK

Take a look at the facing page. It has a sequence of frames that form the pages of a flipbook. In order to build this animation device, you'll need a large paper binder, scissors, and a photocopy of the frame page.

Once you have made a photocopy, use your scissors to cut out each frame. Don't forget the order of the frames. Stack them in the correct sequence and secure the stack together with a paper binder. Make sure that the binder grips the blank side of the frames. Now quickly flip the stack. What do you see? Try flipping the stack backwards. What happens now? How does the flipping speed affect the illusion?

FANTASCOPE

Back in the 1800s, there was no TV, video games, or computers. What did people do?

Many people engaged in a curious pastime called reading. Others played with all sorts of devices called parlor toys. One successful toy was known as the phenakistoscope (pronounced FEN-ah-key-stah-scope). Some people just called it a fantascope.

This toy uses a rotating shutter and a reflected image to produce the illusion of motion. Instead of reading about this toy, why not construct it?

BUILDING A FANTASCOPE

You'll need the following materials to assemble a fantascope:

    Pencil
    Pushpin
    Scissors

1. Photocopy the disk onto a sheet of heavy-stock paper.

NOTE: If the photocopy is done on standard-weight paper, you can always paste it to a backing of heavier stock.

2. Use your scissors to carefully cut out the circular disk shape.

3. Once the disk has been cut, use your scissors to snip out the tiny viewing slots that are found along the disk edge.

4. Insert a pushpin into the center of the disk.

5. Anchor the pushpin into the rubber eraser of a long pencil.

6. The disk should spin freely on its pushpin axle. If it binds, twist the disk back and forth until it spins freely.

7. Stand in front of a mirror. Hold the fantascope so that the printed frames reflect back to you.

8. Look at the reflection of the disk through one of the slots. You should see most if not all of the frame drawings.

9. Keep looking through the slot. Now spin the disk. Don't move. Keep looking at the reflection through this slotted shutter. What do you see?

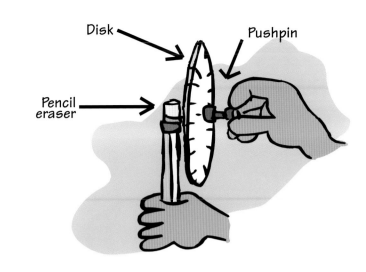

Disk

Pushpin

Pencil
eraser

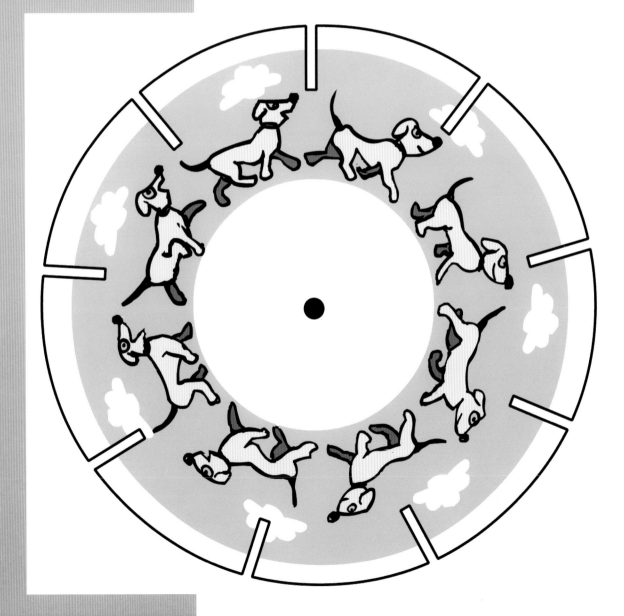

ZOOTROPE

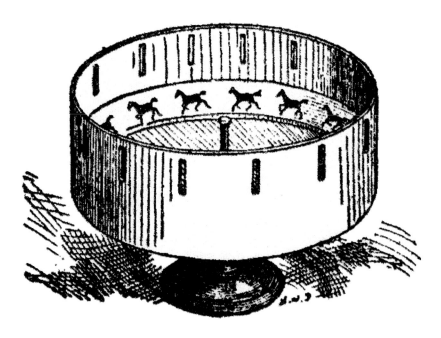

In 1867, a U.S. patent was awarded to an inventor for a device he called the zootrope. Like the fantascope, the zootrope created the illusion of motion. However, instead of depending upon a mirrored reflection, the zootrope uses a slotted, rotating drum.

The word zootrope means "wheel of life." Soon after its release, the zootrope became a very popular parlor toy. New animations could be purchased as a band of frames that was inserted into the drum.

BUILDING A ZOOTROPE

You'll need the following materials to make a zootrope:

Scissors
Tape
Phonograph turntable or lazy Susan

1. Photocopy the two frame sheets on the facing page.

2. Use your scissors to cut them out.

3. Carefully snip out the viewing slots along the upper edge of both strips.

4. Use tape to secure the strips into a large loop. Make sure that the frames are on the inside of the loop.

5. Place the completed loop on the center of a phonograph turntable or lazy Susan.

6. If you're using a turntable, spin it or set it to 33 rpm. If you're using a lazy Susan, simply spin it. With both eyes open, look through the slots at the rotating images. What do you see?

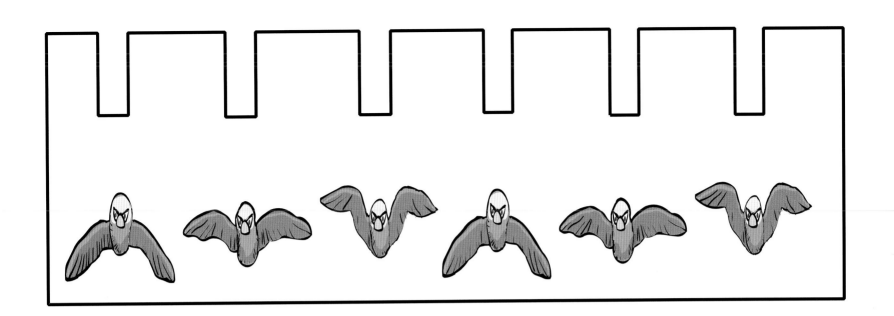

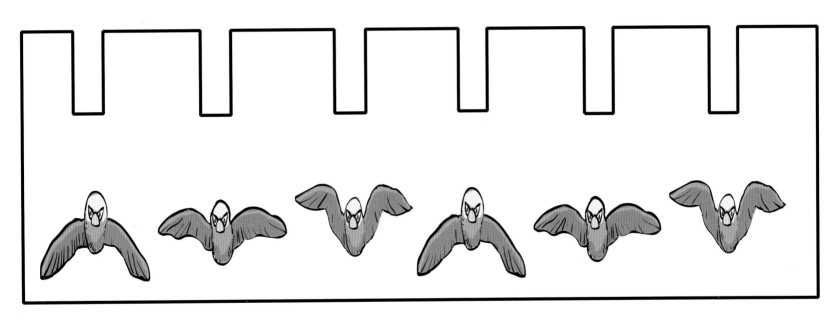

DIVING INTO DEPTH

DEEPER UNDERSTANDING

Did you know that the 3-D world you see is an illusion? It may be a very accurate illusion, but it still is an illusion. How can that be? Isn't the world 3-D? Yes, the world is three-dimensional, but the image that is cast upon your eye is only 2-D.

Your eyes have light-detecting cells called rods and cones, which are embedded in a layer at the back of the eye known as the retina. Although the retina is curved, its surface is mostly flat. This makes it two-dimensional.

The image that is cast upon the retina is also 2-D. Yet your brain uses the images that you obtain from each eye to create the realistic illusion of a 3-D world. The cues taken from these images to construct a 3-D world include:

Overlap: A closer object blocks out a farther object.
Relative speed: Things that are closer appear to move quicker.
Brightness: Closer things appear brighter.
Binocular views: Differences in our right-eye and left-eye views of the world.

OVERLAP

Overlap is a cue that your two eyes use to develop a sense of 3-D. When you overlap a right-eye and left-eye image, your brain throws in some extra processing and "paints" the scene with depth.

Here's how to overlap views:

Position your hands at an arm's distance away. Hold up the index finger of each hand. Separate the hands by about 1 foot. Look at a distant object such as a painting on a wall or a far-off house. Focus and concentrate on that object. Your fingers should take on a ghostly appearance.

Keeping your fingers upright, slowly bring your hands together. At a certain distance, the fingers will overlap each other and form a "double thickness." Keep looking at the distant object. Don't focus on the fingers. If you do, the ghosts will separate and you'll end up seeing two distinct fingers. The overlap that you see is essential for viewing the following illusions.

FREE VIEWING Let these two images below drift towards each other. Begin by relaxing and looking beyond the paper. Pretend the paper is see-through and you are looking at a distant scene. When you focus on a plane beyond the page, the two images will come towards each other.

The ability to fuse these images without any devices is called free viewing. Some people refer to free-viewing as lazy-eyeness. Can you see why?

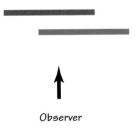

When the images overlap, you'll see a picture in two distinct planes. The square should appear in the front and cover up a part of the more-distant circle.

Here's how the objects of the scene will appear to be positioned if this illusionary arrangement can be seen from above.

Observer

Now that you know what to expect, try fusing this next image. It's a slightly more complex stack, but the final effect is the same. You should see depth where there is no depth.

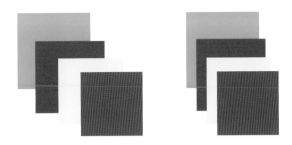

The ability to let the images overlap improves with practice. In fact, it's the same process needed to decode the magic dot images that contain a hidden 3-D scene. The "trick" to being able to overlap images is relaxing. You need to let your focus go "beyond" the page. As you did when overlapping fingers, your focus is set on a distant object, not the fingers. At first, this is difficult to do. All your life you've learned to focus on what you are looking at. Now you need to focus beyond the page.

DRIFTING TOGETHER

Honestly answer this question.

My ability to drift and fuse a right-eye and left-eye image is:

a. Awful.

b. Horrible.

c. Irrelevant. I gave up and jumped ahead to page 76.

If you answered A, B, or C to the above question, we have a tool that will help you.

TUBES THAT FUSE IMAGE PAIRS

Roll up two sheets of paper into tubes. Use your hands to form eyecups at the end of each tube that you'll be looking through. Examine each of the target pairs on these pages with this viewing device. Make sure that each tube has an isolated and separate view. One tube should be centered over the left-eye image. The other tube should be centered over the right-eye image. Relax. In a few seconds the right-eye and left-eye image will drift towards each other and overlap.

TARGET PRACTICE

Here's the first target pair. Position the tubes so that the right and left bull's-eye are isolated from each other and sent to different eyes.

Once the images overlap, your brain will construct a scene in which the central bull's-eye floats above the outer circle. Here's what the illusion looks like if you can see it from the side.

GOING IN

So far our overlapping illusions have produced the appearance of something "jumping" out of the paper. We can also produce an illusion that appears to go into the page. Look at the image below through your tubes.

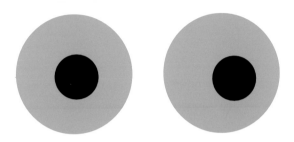

Many people will construct a scene in which the dark core of these circles is farther away than the outer blue shape. This "reversed" illusion is also produced by overlap.

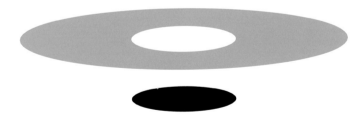

So why doesn't the inner core pop forward? It has to do with the distance between the overlapping shapes. At certain distances, the overlap produces the appearance of a target that rises above the plane of the paper. At other separation distances, the overlap suggests an illusion in which the target shape appears below the paper plane.

SIDE TRICK

Hold this book at eye level. Then position your nose at the "Place your nose here" mark. Look at the X. Does anything strange happen to this X?

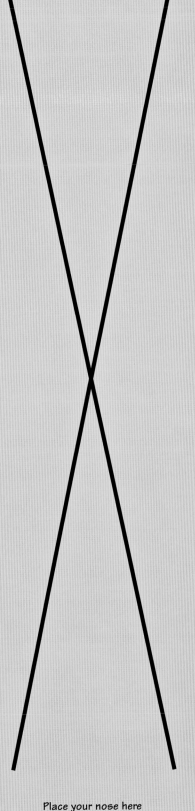

The X appears to grow an extra line. This imaginary line is caused by the crossing over of each eye's vision field. This crossover creates a reinforced ghostly image that takes on the appearance of a central third line.

Place your nose here

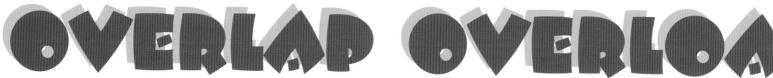

OVERLAP OVERLOAD

DOT DITTO DEMYSTIFIED Relax and overlap these rows of images. If you can't free view this effect, use paper tubes to help fuse the image pairs. What do you see?

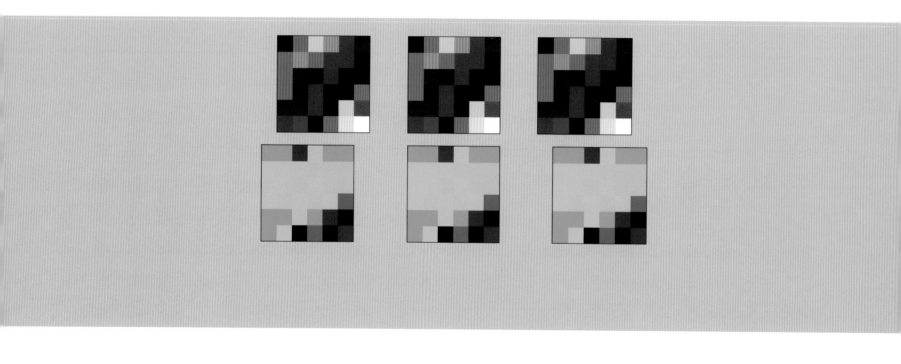

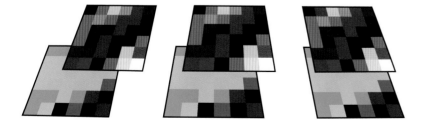

The squares overlap and produce the illusion of 3-D. Keep examining the scene. To most people, the upper row of three squares appears to float somewhat higher than the lower row. This difference in percieved height is caused by the difference in separation distance.

The squares of the upper row are closer together. The squares in the lower row are wider apart. When the squares in both rows are overlapped, this difference between the images creates the illusion of different planes.

STEREOGRAM Take a look at the "random" dot stereoimage below. Can you see a pattern within the jumble of dots?

Locate the two black dots at the top of this dot image. They are there to help you get the focus plane of this illusion. Free view these two dots so they overlap. Once the dots overlap, a ghostly third dot will appear. At that time, look below and you'll see the 3-D image that is hidden in the jumble of dots.

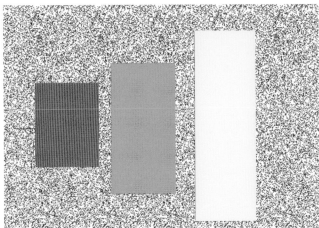

The pattern that is embedded into the dot placement is a very simple arrangement of rectangles. This basic view is easier to see than the more complex stereodot images. Here's what the pop-up pattern looks like.

Vantage Advantage

Before we begin looking at right-eye and left-eye photographs, let's have a better understanding of why we see a different view from each eye. Look at the drawing below (with both eyes). You'll see the position of target in which the right edge appears closer to the observer than the left edge.

We've included lines that show the paths of light that reach the eyes from the target. These rays help show the difference in the target's appearance observed by each eye.

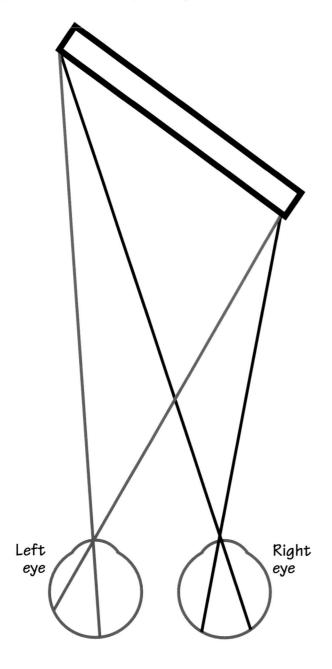

As you can see, the right eye and left eye see slightly different views. The left eye looks more directly at the target and captures a longer and more straight-on image of it. In contrast, the right eye has a more angled view. Its image of the target is more "squished" than the other eye's view.

Left
eye

Right
eye

WHAT WE SEE
Looking at the target, each eye captures a slightly different view of it as shown at the right.

Apply your free viewing technique on these two images. Relax. As these images fuse together, your brain goes at it again and creates the illusion of depth. If needed, use your viewing tubes to help achieve this effect.

Left-eye view　　　*Right-eye view*

A THIRD TARGET
People often find it easier to see these illusions when presented with three targets. Although one target is a repeat, it offers a shape on which to focus your attention. Try looking at these targets with your free viewing technique. Does the middle book cover more easily pop into 3-D?

STEREO- PHOTOS

Here's a stereophoto pair that has been printed onto a heavy-stock card. To see the illusion, insert the card into a stereoscope.

For over 100 years, photographers have "played" with the magic of 3-D illusions by using images called stereoviewer cards, stereoviews, stereoscopic photos, or stereophotos.

Unlike a regular image, a stereophoto consists of two side-by-side views. Although it may not be apparent at first glance, these views present a distinct and slightly different right-eye and left-eye vantage.

Stereophotos are usually found on heavy-stock cardboard. This sturdy card is inserted into a viewer called a stereoscope. The card is moved closer or farther away until its images are in focus. When each eye receives its own separate and unique view, the brain completes the job by fusing the images into a 3-D scene.

VIEWING WITHOUT A VIEWER

Take a look at the stereophotos on the opposite page. If you don't have a stereoscope, there are several ways for you to see the 3-D magic of these image pairs.

UNAIDED VIEW

This technique requires no tools, but it is the most difficult way to experience the effect. To attain success and minimal frustration, you should be very skilled at free viewing (see pages 64–65). You may want to practice on simple overlaps before applying this technique to stereophotos. Remember to relax. Do not focus on the stereophotos, but instead look beyond these images. Let the right-hand and left-hand photo drift together. Once they overlap, explore this 3-D scene, but don't refocus on the plain of the page.

TUBE VIEW

This technique is covered on pages 66–67. Simply roll up two tubes of paper. View each image of the pair through one of the tubes. Relax. The images have a long distance to drift before they overlap.

HAND LENS VIEWER

Obtain two inexpensive magnifying lenses. Hold each lens several inches above the stereophotos to focus these images. Move your face close to these lenses. When a separate in-focus image arrives at each eye, your brain does the rest and creates the illusion of depth.

INTRO TO RED/BLUE 3-D

You've most likely seen a red and blue 3-D image. They look abstract, but when viewed with a pair of red/blue 3-D glasses, the image magically pops out at you. The red/blue 3-D illusions are called anaglyphs (pronounced: ANNA-gliffs).

WHAT'S THE TRICK? Anaglyphs depend upon the colors of light, not the focusing ability of lenses, to separate the target images. Each finished anaglyph consists of two images—a red one and a blue one. The red image is the right-eye view. The blue image is the left-eye view. And as you've seen, these two views are printed on top of each other.

When you put on the red/blue viewing glasses, the filters allow only one of the printed colors to reach each eye.

RED FILTER The red filter keeps out the blue. Since blue light can't pass through this filter, your eye can't detect this color. Therefore, any blue in the target image is seen as black. The rest of the image takes on a red tint.

BLUE FILTER The blue filter keeps out the red. Since red light can't pass through this filter, your eye can't detect this color. Therefore, any red in the target image is seen as black. The rest of the image takes on a blue tint.

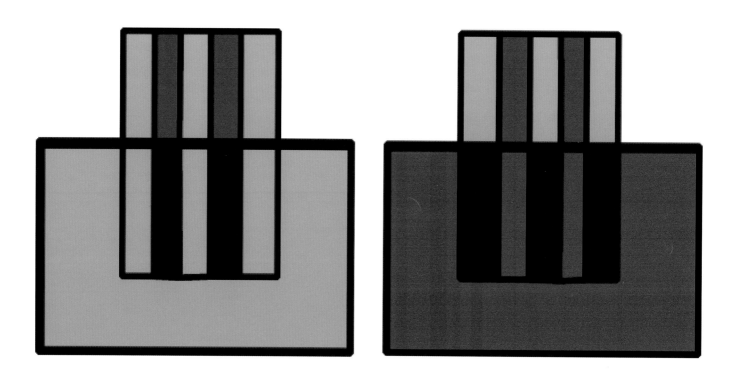

VIEWING GLASSES You probably have a crumpled viewer tucked away in your junk pile, or inserted between the pages of a 3-D comic book. If you can't find one, you can create your own by holding a sheet of blue plastic (from report covers) over your right eye and red plastic over your left eye. Then look at the anaglyph of the Golden Gate Bridge above.

MAKING ANAGLYPHS

You can create your own private library of anaglyphs. Here's what you need:

Desktop computer

Camera (you don't need a camera if you want to create red/blue anaglyphs from stereophoto cards)

Scanner (only needed if you are using photographic prints or old stereoviews)

Photo processing software, such as the expanded version of Adobe Photoshop® that can merge color together

NOTE: The menu options in your version of Photoshop may differ from the ones described in the steps below. Don't hesitate to check your software manual for more details.

1. Obtain a pair of stereophotos by taking two pictures of the same scene. You don't need a special camera to take these pictures. On the second shot, make sure to move your camera to the right by several inches. This will produce a pair of images with a right-eye and left-eye view.

2. Create a separate file for each of the two images. If you are using a digital camera, this automatically occurs when the images are downloaded into the computer. If you are using a film camera, you'll first need to develop and print the film. Then scan the photographs into your computer and save each as an image file.

Here's a stereophoto that was taken with an ordinary film camera. If you look at the flag, you'll see that these two images were not captured at the same instant. Instead, they were taken several seconds apart. For the right image, the camera was held a few inches to the side.

3. Lose the color of the images by turning them into grayscale. Once the color information is lost, resave the image in RGB (red, green, blue) mode.

4. Strip away the red color (or channel) from the left-hand image by opening it in Photoshop. Highlight this picture. Under the menu option "Window," select "Show Channels." Drag your mouse to choose "Red Channel" and "Cut" the selection.

Although you won't see a separate colorized image in the anaglyph-making process, these pictures illustrate the separation of red/blue views. Look at this image pair with your red/blue glasses. Shut one eye. Which image can you see? What happens to the other image? Now view this pair with the other eye. What happens now? Can you see how this process sends only one color to each eye?

5. Copy the red channel information of the right-hand image in Photoshop by highlighting the right-hand image. Under the menu option "Window," select "Show Channels." Drag your mouse to choose "Red Channel" and "Copy" this selection.

6. Paste the red channel data into the left-hand image by going to it. Under the menu option "Window," select "Show

Channels." Drag your mouse to choose "Red Channel" and "Paste" the image information.

7. Under the menu option "Window," select "Show Channels." Drag your mouse to choose "RGB Channel" and all of the anaglyph colors will appear.

In order to see the image in 3-D, you need to view the finished anaglyph with red/blue decoding glasses. Make sure that the blue lens is over your right eye.

MEGA AND MICRO VIEWS

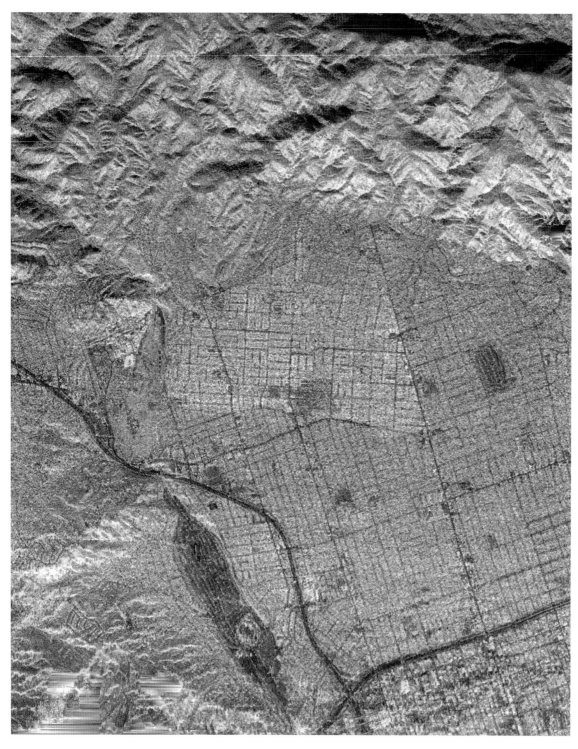

Did you know that stereophoto pairs are used by map makers to chart the height of places? Take a look at the image on the left. This is a view of Pasadena in California from outer space. The anaglyph image was created from stereophotos captured by a high-flying camera. Compare the ups and downs of the cityscape with the surrounding mountains.

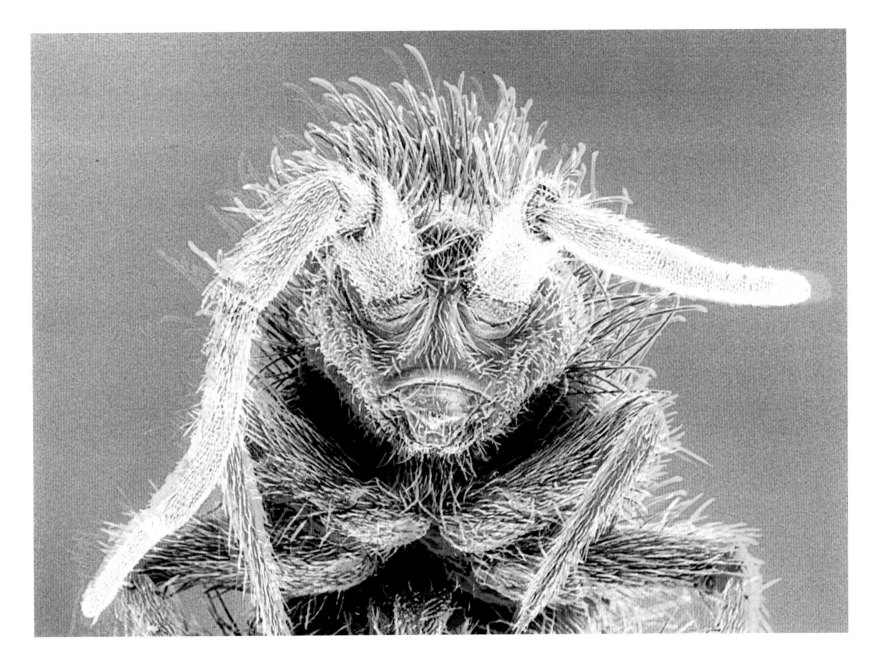

MICROSCOPIC MONSTER

The bug above is called a springtail. This 3-D image was created by David Burder, one of the world's experts in 3-D photography.

ABOUT THE AUTHOR

Michael Anthony DiSpezio is a renaissance educator who teaches, writes, and conducts teacher workshops throughout the world. He is the author of CRITICAL THINKING PUZZLES, GREAT CRITICAL THINKING PUZZLES, CHALLENGING CRITICAL THINKING PUZZLES, VISUAL THINKING PUZZLES, AWESOME EXPERIMENTS IN ELECTRICITY AND MAGNETISM, AWESOME EXPERIMENTS IN FORCE AND MOTION, AWESOME EXPERIMENTS IN LIGHT AND SOUND, OPTICAL ILLUSION MAGIC, and SIMPLE OPTICAL ILLUSION EXPERIMENTS WITH EVERYDAY MATERIALS (all from Sterling). He is also the co-author of over two dozen elementary, middle, and high school science textbooks and has been a "hired creative-gun" for clients including The Weather Channel and Children's Television Workshop. He also develops activities for the classroom guides to DISCOVER magazine and SCIENTIFIC AMERICAN FRONTIERS.

Michael was a contributor to the National Science Teachers Association's Pathways to Science Standards. This document set offers guidelines for moving the national science standards from vision to practice. Michael's work with the NSTA has also included authoring the critically acclaimed NSTA curriculum, THE SCIENCE OF HIV.

Index